THE AQUA NOTEBOOK

TASHA COTTER

ANAPHORA LITERARY PRESS

QUANAH, TEXAS

ANAPHORA LITERARY PRESS
1108 W 3rd Street
Quanah, TX 79252
https://anaphoraliterary.com

Book design by Anna Faktorovich, Ph.D.

Printed in the United States of America, United Kingdom and in Australia on acid-free paper.

Edited by: Salim Dharamshi

Published in 2019 by Anaphora Literary Press

The Aqua Notebook
Tasha Cotter—1st edition.

Library of Congress Control Number: 2018954268

Library Cataloging Information
Cotter, Tasha, 1984-, author.
    The aqua notebook / Tasha Cotter
    80 p. ; 9 in.
    ISBN 978-1-68114-466-5 (softcover : alk. paper)
    ISBN 978-1-68114-467-2 (hardcover : alk. paper)
    ISBN 978-1-68114-468-9 (e-book)
1. Poetry—American—General. 2. Poetry—Women Authors.
3. Biography & Autobiography—Literary Figures.
PN6099-6110: Collections of general literature: Poetry
811: American poetry in English

THE AQUA NOTEBOOK

TASHA COTTER

January 24th

The black cat is coiled in a messy ball
On my lap, and it feels like we've been
Snowed in for weeks, though it's only been
Three days. I've been stocking the birdfeeders
With sunflower seed, and playing with the dog
In the snowy yard. You are re-organizing
The kitchen again. You've baked us bread,
And cured your own bacon.
We're snowed in together. The dog is now
Sleeping in the other room. I can hear
One cat in the kitchen; the other licks
And licks her long white fur. She stops
To glance out the window behind us,
And continues taking a bath, as if she, too,
Is content to spend the day with us, like this.

January 26, 2016

I want to remember this winter:
The wordless white at dawn
That gave no hint of what was
To come, early on. My life has begun
To figure itself out. No one said it,
They didn't have to. I know there is
A part of me that has cooled off,
But will never go completely cold.
Heavy as the cloud of white
Weather that's paused outside
My window, I'm softly, breaking
Through, my arms full of wordless
Things. I am not a storm. I never
Was. They called off school
Because of a predicted storm
And so today, at first, felt like a gift.
Then: silence. We are at that part
Of the season: the suspended quiet
Of disbelief that lasts just a minute
Before the head-rush of spring.
The clipped call of a bird, I heard,
Before you left felt like an important
Thing was being said in the bushes.
I wanted a new view of winter,
So I asked this poem: What is it
My wrens know, that I don't?
The dog, a little watch-man at the door
Stares at the world gone heavy with snow.
It is all too still and too blank for her.
There is no one for miles, nothing
To quicken her heart. No pairs
Of people for her to consider. We retreat
Into our home, the only movement,

A staggered line of gray chimney smoke
Thin and then out of sight. We stay
Locked in all weekend, wondering
When the snow will melt, as if life,
Couldn't really be life until it did.

February 7th

Tonight, a feast
Of roast chicken and vegetables,
Dinner at the dining room table
And making plans among the quiet,
Tiny heartbreaks that we bear
Together. Tonight, getting ready
For tomorrow's Monday rush,
I thought, we are alive.
We are not dead. And I know
That because this is our life, here,
Right now: happy and busy,
Dish towel in hand.
This is the house we live in
Right now, in our thirties.
These are our two cats,
And this is our one dog
Who likes to sit patiently in
The middle of the kitchen
While meals are being cooked.
These are the lights we turn
Off before bed and this is
The time we go to bed on nights
Before we go to work.
I'm telling you this here
Because I didn't tell you earlier:
I was happy, flipping off the light
To go upstairs. It felt like closing
The chapter of a very good book.
I'm always happy and surprised,
By you, by us. Even when we talk
About the things we'd change
If we could. I wouldn't change
Much. I never knew what I wanted.

Tonight I discovered what I discover
Each day: all along I wanted this
Exact miraculous thing.

February 8th

I like the way you can take
A song and connect it to your life.
I'm thinking of the heartbreaks,
Humming along to a song
I know by heart. My mother
Once danced with my baby brother
In her arms while I stood, a little girl,
Watching as they danced to 'Eternal
Flame' by The Bangles. All the world
Seemed to stop in that moment
And so I know why I remember it:
It was the first time I felt in love
With life and where I come from.
With songs, I like how I can almost
Know everything that ever
Existed. I can get a sense
Of myself through everyone else.
There's a story to every person,
And behind every love story
Exists another story that's never told.

February 9th

You will go without alcohol.
You will go without meat, you said,
Lent begins tomorrow and already
You are making plans to go downtown
To confession. You sit alone, jotting down
Notes and when I ask you what they're
About you tell me you're writing down
Notes to have at confession. I nod
And ask no more questions, but I wonder
What you're thinking and what you're writing.
I want to know, and I could probably ask,
But it feels like your private thoughts,
Or your private wishes and fears. What's there
To be sorry for? What's weighing on you?
I wonder, too, if you feel something like this
When it's you sitting across the room, watching
As I write things down that I can't say aloud.
Maybe you, too, wonder what it's all about.

February 12th

Today the gray and cold won't budge
From the charred roads. We are all deep
In this winter. All still and observant,
Poised for spring. Last night I was sick,
Still coughing, still under a blanket
With a book I received for Christmas:
A biography big as a brick by Hermione Lee
On Virginia Woolf. For an hour I forgot
The cold, and my own sore throat.
It took me back to reading *Orlando*
When I was twenty-years-old.
How the book spun me around,
And how I felt dazzled by Woolf's
Imagination. The book was an event
In my young life, and for a long time
I wasn't sure if I liked Virginia Woolf
Or not. I read *Mrs. Dalloway* as an
Eighteen-year-old and hated it.
I re-read it when I was twenty-six
And fell in love, wondering who I was
To hate the book in the first place.
But probably, the best thing I read last
Night was how she wrote extensively
In her diaries, sorting her soul away
From the experience of living. I liked
Reading how she talked about
Herself endlessly. She wrote letters
To others, and the letters were full
Of her, or else, she'd attend dinner
Parties and ask someone seven
Or ten questions in a row, not waiting
For a response. People said
Her life gave her little material,

So she had to get her material
From others. And perhaps, my favorite
Bit so far was the one and only time
She met Freud. It was in 1939.
He greeted her with a narcissus.

February 14th

Out the window, the icy cold
Twilight—a silencing of everything.
Only the occasional chirps of local birds
Coming in low for seed. The new snow
Is falling and the world feels steeped
In the vast silence of a winter Sunday.
The record cold is the only thing
Anyone is talking about. Today
I lit some jasmine incense
And spent some time with my book
On Virginia Woolf. I set out three
Terracotta saucers on the front porch,
And filled each with a different blend
Of millet and seed. It's something I learned
From my grandmother as a young girl:
The need to look beyond yourself in endless
Winter, even when your heart draws a blank
On Valentine's Day, and you know you're free
But you'd swear, you're locked in a cage.

February 18th

I like to sit at the enormous Intermezzo bar
At lunch with all the beautiful campus girls'
Heads bent, their eyes fixed on celebrities
On their screens. The girls are perched
Like downy birds, each in a winter coat
And we hover far above the heads
Of others who are coming in from the cold,
Hurrying into the building, tucking themselves
Into the collars of their coats. From here, you can
Hide in plain sight and I wonder if that's why
They do it, all meeting here like a secret
Society each day at lunch. Some of the passersby
Look up at us, if only for a second.
The girls don't notice. The girls have earbuds
In their ears. The girls are now scrolling
Through another girls four-hundred
Photos on Facebook. Still, I sit with them
In silence. It's Thursday afternoon, and a mood
I can't identify is infecting all of us as I watch
the show going on below us, on Earth.

February 21st

It was a dinner of salmon, zucchini,
And hot and sour soup. Imagine
How I felt when they began talking
About me without you. Candles
Were lit. I began to lower my head,
Suddenly too warm in my sweater.
What is the point of imagining me,
Alone, in the home we live in?
And what could ever happen
To you? Why ask questions
About the deed and whose name
Is on what? Why would I think
Of living in the same room
We read in and made plans.
I refuse to imagine there will never be you
Across from me, carefully folding
The paper back, your stack of books
On the table to your right, reading
As the sun sets in front of us,
The peach fire we see each night.
Why would I want to think about
That kind of absence, as if that
Absence could ever be a part
Of this house. No, I can't allow
That stranger into the house.

February 24th

I like watching winter turn to spring,
Feel the shift of time rearrange the constellation
of us. We exist in our respective orbits
Where we live in separate leagues.
There's a dailiness to these wilderness years
That reminds me of who we were.
The past branches off, ends in a green
Bud—as if that end was what was meant
To happen all along. We didn't know
It would do that, did we? The ground
Under my boots is sure winter
Is about to release. I step, crunching
The ground into a thousand tiny voices
Made of glass until the barely living
Earth is visible. Are you listening?
The red flowers are humming,
Their green bulbs are covered in clay mud.
The clouds pass and the wind is still.
The blank sky leaves a phantom quiet,
And for a moment, I've been left behind.
I get this way, melancholy, watching
Seasons change. Why did we change?
We tried so hard not to. I think
We'll always be dying for something
And we'll always be getting born
Again, in the daylight. Today, I'll open
My eyes and promise you I'll be new
At this life. I'll be a pioneer. A poet
Asking spring: teach me everything.

March 2nd

Last night, looking up from the book
You were reading, you told me about the man
Who became a wild animal in his sleep.
His wife woke to him on the bedroom floor, growling,
On all fours. He destroyed their hardwood
Floor with his bare hands. His fingertips bled
And bled and yet, he went back to bed,
This half man, half animal. He slept
It all off, or so it seemed to her. The next
Morning, he didn't remember anything.
You looked to me, then. I said I didn't believe
He was possessed, like the book was claiming
He was. A true story, you assured me.
Maybe drugs? I asked, sitting across from you,
At eight o'clock on a work night, blanket
Wrapped around my lap, but you got quiet.
You said it couldn't be drugs, could it?
Then I got quiet, too, wondering where you were
Going. You furrowed your brow and told me
The book is nonfiction; what does it mean
That a man can become a panther
For an hour or two? You said, you don't know
How to make sense of what you've read
Because the stories all seem like ghost stories
And you never believed in any of that
And I quietly admitted, before going back
To my own book, that I always did.

March 3rd

Today I drove to Springfield, Kentucky.
An hour's drive in the cold, intermittent snow.
The world, gray as it contracted and released
In quick, breaking bursts of light. I found a school
Set way off from the road, high on a grassy hill,
A dark, cloudy pond at the base. I love
These small community colleges I find
Nestled in the hills of this state: the people
Helping people. The coffee that was brewed
Hours ago. The clean, quiet halls. The people
Welcoming me and telling me what they know;
The Dodge trucks and cattle trailers I see
Parking outside of the front office window.
The industrial maintenance lab, the elaborate
Machines cleaned and ready, their tiny lights
Blinking white. There are some students here
Who want to study business. I watch
Three students file into a computer lab
And as soon as I think I know what to expect
A girl I've never seen before walks up to me,
Smiling. She tells me she likes writing;
Asks me if there's anything I can do to help.

March 6th

The house is steeped in a white light
Marble stillness. The cats, the dog,
All sit, eyes closed with their faces
To the sun as if they've fallen into some
Late winter afternoon trance, and I think
They're right: Heat is that comforting.
Or maybe they're all dreaming
Of the coming spring. Maybe they're
Envisioning green grass; the windows
Opened to allow the breeze to blow
Through the house, the curtains
Fluttering, the floor warm beneath
Their paws. I like that the crowds are gone
And this peace remains: a glass of orange
Juice. A book and some paper. And this
Pen to sort out what's been haunting me.
There's a pressure I know
Well when words go unwritten. It's
As if the universe is checking in on me,
Asking me what I'm doing, reminding me
To never forget some secret task.

March 8th

A seventy degree day
And the girls stand together,
A group of five at the bus stop
In front of the library. They're
Talking, sometimes laughing.
One can't help but sway,
From side to side like she wants
To be dancing. I wonder if they're
Going to a party, but I think,
Probably not at five after five
On a Tuesday afternoon.
They correct a boy for whistling
At them as he walks past. A girl
Calls after him, do you think
I'm an animal? Do you see me
Walking on all fours? He walks
Over and apologizes to all
Of them. The word Hazze
Is tattooed on his neck.
When they are satisfied,
He walks away and they erupt
In a fit of giggles and laughter.
They're trying to figure out
His name. One says she thought
His name was Hades, but no,
It couldn't be that because who
Would ever name their baby that?

March 13th

Who knew your absence would leave
A startling thing? This vacancy, a present
Lack of you. On the news, this morning,
They announced seven days until spring.
The winter is unbecoming now: a dome
Of cloud cover, a reflecting pool of gray rain.
Yet, the Christmas cactus is blooming again—
The knock-out fuchsia has risen up like a flame,
Invisibly recording the world from its perch
On the chipped window ledge; taking in
The earthly cues, it survives and survives.
I want to tell you how the ground is being courted
By spring. How, when I was running through
The country the buttercups and crocuses gave voice
To something buried in me: a memory
From another Sunday: my father, stopping
Along the roadside on the way home from church
To pick daffodils for my mother. That happened.
I nearly forgot the simple happiness of sitting
In the passenger seat as that moment became
Part of me. The day opened up, the beauty
Came through. My eyes filled with white
Afternoon light. What I mean is spring is its own
Form of kindness. It gave me back something
I forgot I once had. And who would we be
Without that kind breaking open of life?

March 21st

There is war. And then there is what you hear
Of war: The Nazi plane that crashed in a neighboring
English village held four dead Nazi's when the locals
Got to the wreckage. The bodies were dragged out
Of the fiery hot metal, the crowds gathered
In the clouds of smoke, their feet quickening
On the burnt grass. Some people watched
As others stomped the heads of the dead
German pilots onto the ruptured ground.
Virginia's work became fragmentary—
And yet she wrote all of this down in bolts
Of lightning on the page. Ideas in the margins
Resembled a rain shower, or a poem titled
'It is Raining', in which the tears are not raining
From your heart, but inside your heart.
On the page where once she sketched plans
For *Orlando* and *Mrs. Dalloway* she left
Behind two suicide notes. The new war
Reminded her of the first war, her break-
Down, the rest cures that never worked,
And besides, the peace was so brief
Between the fighting. What struck me most
Were her letters: one to Leonard, one to Vanessa.
The broken blank space of a woman. The slow
Marching away one morning to the River Ouse,
Where she paused to put some stones in her pockets.
A couple people saw her, thought nothing of it.
She wore her fur coat and she knew how to swim,
At the coroner, it was discovered her watch stopped
At 11:45 in the morning. This is how you go missing.

March 23rd

Against all odds
And the oncoming traffic,
There you are, crossing
The street—illegally.
Ablaze with new words,
As if the daylight
Has given you something
To tell me. Call out
What you need to say.
I want to hear words fly
In the wind tunnels
Of the soaring buildings
Around us. Here there's a love
That winds itself like a bus
Through the streets. It moves
Like the blood running
Through your hands. All paths
Lead to you. Call this feeling
Another name for the sun.
When a woman loves a man
She'll be the driver.
And if she's the driver
She'll know all the places
To stop. She'll know
To be fast, and watch
The clock. Minutes pass.
She's given a warning.
She knows somewhere
Out there, there's you.

March 30th

Looking out the airplane window, a land
I remember. California, you are the giant.
The clouds pass, waving us in and we fly on
Toward LAX. Landing, we take the Pacific Coast
Highway to where we are staying in Rolling Hills,
But not before taking a drive through Rancho
Palos Verdes—a town on the LA peninsula.
I already love the whale watchers, all huddled
At Point Vicente Lighthouse with their expensive
Tripod binoculars: Nikon and Swarovski. I love
How they look and look. Pause to discuss
What was seen yesterday. They have charts
On display. You can read the kind of whales
They've seen. Their eyes move from their notes
To their crystal lenses and they regard this place
The way I do: lucid and frozen from too much
Beauty. My mind hasn't caught up to where it is
And what I'm seeing. I'm watching for the animal
To surface from the deep, catching its breath.

April 2nd

I was sitting on a wooden bench
Overlooking the Pacific Ocean
When I heard the bells ringing: four chimes
Coming from the Wayfarer's Chapel
Announcing it is 8:45 in the morning.
I spent the sunrise with the waves crashing
Against the rocky coast. From here I can see
The distant roads spanning out.
The sounds of fast cars are picking up now,
Reminding me I, too, will be leaving soon.
This moment, too, will fall away
And the colors will change. I'll forget
The family walking the path in front of me,
The little girl to my left calling, "daddy, look!"
Then, after no answer, "mommy ... look!"
I hope I never forget what sixty degrees feels like
On an April day in California, or the warm light
That flooded the glass chapel when I walked inside,
And took a seat in an empty pew. How I closed my eyes.

April 6th

There are some days I'm not a Poet.
On those days I keep it all to myself:
The noise, the people, and emails …
I add the appointment to my Outlook
Calendar. Let me see if I can figure out
What went wrong and get back to you,
I tell the world, ten times an hour.
Tell me again, the university you attend.
Have you seen my red pen?
I have an endless to-do list.
I accept the small piece of candy
Offered to me. And I check my voicemail
Writing down numbers and names.
But these things don't call back to me.
I do my job and get rinsed free
Of feeling. The messiness that is in me
Still hides underneath. Sitting at my desk
I know something's missing. A world
Formed inside my head begs
And begs. It has everything to do
With the invisible people I've met,
And all the things I've still not told you.

April 11th

No poems in me today. The room fills
With the slow sounds of an evening rain,
And there's a new offer on our first home,
But we don't know what to say, the offer
Nearly sinks us both. The home is getting older,
There's a crack in its foundation. Too many
Times now, we've had buyers back out.
It was the place we bought before we were
Even married. We watched *The Office* on NBC
From the red couch. We planted the asparagus
Bed. We watched a maple tree get planted
In the front yard. I'm aware these things don't
Matter to anyone but us. And yet,
It matters. No one cares that we designed
The kitchen to remind us of our honeymoon
In Sicily. Of Palermo and Trapani. The truth is
I'm not even sure we were happy in that home.
I'm glad we got out of that place. The dark rooms,
The narrow hallway. Maybe the place whispers its truth.

April 18th

Some days the poems are above you,
Hiding in the trees. The summer air
Taunts you, the voices of the people
Seem to say, there's poetry here,
Don't you see it? It's waiting for you
If only you knew what to do
With all this beauty on the page.
But where to begin? There's a girl
Beside me wearing pearls to the gym.
Her glossy pink pedicure shines
in the sunlight. For a little while
All I can think about is color
And pearls. Pink and black: why are they
This thing I have fallen into
On this day that reminds me of summer
In the way a summer day makes us
Sense an element of chance, electric
And alive and racing through the air,
So fast, you can't see it.
And you think, *how wild all this is.*
Maybe this is how it really is:
You are there, built into this world
Of black and brightness, pink and white.

April 20th

Let me tell you about the brick buildings
And the sidewalks. The Kentucky Native
Cafe and the red plaid couch you can see
In the upstairs window of Chatham's
Southern Comfort Food restaurant. The street
Sweepers. The bus drivers. The latecomers.
The freshmen boys listening to Drake
In their Dodge Dakotas. The yellow
Dresses and hair wraps. People waiting
On benches in eighty degrees. It's spring.
How anyone can turn away from life
On a day like today. My heart beats its wings
In my chest. Everything is competing
For the chance to be seen. I don't know
If I have deep beliefs. Or convictions.
But I'm here and I'm alive and I love
How the windows of this city are filled
With the bright faces of flowers, poised,
Framed in color, seeming to see me.

April 25th

I spent my weekend with my poetry
Sisters. They remind me I'm not alone
In my amazement and bewilderment.
It was so nice to meet you there, reader.
You were there at the Book Fair.
I saw you turning the words over like stones.
Someone said that if I like caves, then I should read
Ultima Thule. Poets, we are all related
By our passions and our family library.
How we all need to occasionally be deep
Within our tribe of writers to remember
What we're doing here, our pens on the page
Assembling a new language from letters
As if waiting for a spark to catch fire.
How else to glimpse a life, the stretching dark
We exist in as these fires start and stop.

April 26th

Last night I dreamed
I was the only person alive who remembered
To bring an umbrella on a day that it rained
Throughout the entire world. Was it the sunshine
And perfect weather that made everyone else think
There was no chance of an afternoon shower?
In the dream it rained hard for two minutes
And I was there, taking it all in. It was pure
Joy watching people laugh and walk, then run
To shelter, and it was still a sunny day,
Despite everything. The scent of rain rose up
From the ground and that, too, I liked.
And all the while I knew the rain would stop.
I knew I didn't have long until the spell would be
Broken. The world would take on its old color.
But the thing I remember most about the dream
Was how it felt to be the only one who knew a secret
Ending would come to carry us from this mystery;
That the sky had planned to release us all
Along and that the end would come after I was
Done being witness to the dancing here on earth.

May 1st

We are rushing into the future
Of our tenth year together and we've
Decided to frame the images of places
We've been and where we come from:
Mammoth Cave National Park,
Mount Desert Island and Frenchman Bay.
Natural Bridge, Kentucky, and just this
Year The South Coast Botanic Garden
In Rancho Palos Verdes, California—
A tropical garden, on the LA peninsula.
It seems like the right thing to do:
To travel, to frame what you may not
Fully remember one day.
The past anchored onto the present,
Maybe this is how a house becomes
A home. Maybe this is what it's like to grow
Old with each other.
I'm surprised by where we've been.
In the middle of this spring thunderstorm,
A weather warning interrupts the soft drizzle
Of background music and this day
Stretches past me, filling the living room.

May 4th

I want to write a poem for the southern
Kentucky spring, an ode to the Blue-Eyed
Marys, the Violets, Bloodroot and trees
I stop to stare at; their blooms impossibly
Rich and fragile. The pink blooms of trees
Rush to the ground with every rain shower,
How it almost hurts your chest to walk
Over their strewn bodies, a thousand of them,
Under the soles of your shoes. I love these
Wildflowers: The Blue Lobelias
That carpet the ground, reminding me
Of natural beauty all over again. I like
The innocence of the Fire Pink flower,
It's open mouth electric as a miniature tropical
Star, caught, frozen in the landscape.
The Larkspur ruptures the stillness
And quiet that haunted us for so long.
Did we forget the world was just waiting
To bring out the Phlox and Purple
Phacelia? How soft the world still is
With its Redbuds and White Violets,
Its Anemones whose skin is as white
And pure as a nightgown. Nestled
In the Stonecrop, the Trout Lilies
Trumpet and tilt up so animated I swear
In some other dimension they are alive
And roaring with sound. Who could
Have imagined we're here, walking
With poppies and Shooting Stars?

May 10th

Today I went to look for my notes
That I took for a poem. Notes I wrote
While stuck on Buchanan Avenue
In Asheville, with you. After the car broke
Down, after we got locked out
Of the house and spent an hour
Waiting for roadside assistance
To tow the car to a nearby garage.
Sitting there, for an hour, watching
The wrens land nearby on a wire,
The sun and air soft with afternoon
Water and light, you could almost
Hear the mint growing in the barrels
That lined the walkway. The moment
Seemed to me one more thing
That we'll look back on, recalling
The day when too many things went
Wrong. We sat there, in silence, sensing
A disaster, both not wanting to admit it
And give the moment that kind of power.
I've learned I can wait wordless
For hours, and keep watch,
If you need me to, as you stew
And think, impatience gripping you
By the throat, as you plan your escape.
I can tell how time has shaped us,
Bent us like the necks of all the tangled
North Carolina flowers that surrounded
Us in their search for light. I wonder
What it is that's angled our hearts
Toward the same thing we can't see,
But which we know exists.

May 16th

Lately, I've been looking outside
Of everything I know, scouting around
For clues. I find myself under a dome
Of stained glass, a prayer, a feeling
Of thanks in my chest. I'm turning toward
Subjects I've not thought about
In many years: themes of inspiration,
Ideas of devotion. I flip through books
Questioning God. Letting myself be
Open to something, I realize, I never was.
I want to know something—anything
About transformation. I'm going
In search of heaven and hell, indulging
My foggy understanding of religious
Rituals. You catch me reading
A memoir on grief, deep in
The religious aisle. I pick up
An atlas, study the map of Sodom
And Gomorrah. I recall all those
Long-ago Sundays, sitting around
A small wooden table, the teacher
Leading Sunday school, and the Bible
Trivia game we always played
At the end of every lesson. I was
Never sure of anything. Never thought
Too much about the stories I was taught
As a seven-year-old girl but I suspected
That anything could be real.
I won the trivia game, always. I could memorize
Anything after a while. I don't know what it means
To be wondering about all those parables
Now after putting it all away. Don't know
What it means to be looking for something
To have faith in when I was always the runaway.

May 19th

I call my mother right after I leave work,
Five days a week, and it's not just
To hear the run-down of what she had
For lunch, or breakfast, what she did
At the YMCA or even how my brother's
Been doing in graduate school
On the east coast. No, it's more about
The sound of her voice, her presence
While not present. The conversation
Is easy and predictable, and it lasts
From the time I reach the Chemistry-
Physics building until I pass
The university library, looming large
On the hill. Ten minutes, maybe,
Is as long as we speak. I'm always
Surprised by her laughter. I noticed
It today: her bright, honest laughter
At the small things—minor tragedies—
Things anyone else would find irritating
My mother laughs at, as if to say
That's life. And I smile to myself, knowing
She can handle anything. Before the phone call ends
She'll tell me some rumor she's heard;
Throws in a little gossip for good measure.
And I never tell her I'm glad we can
talk like this. I listen. She talks. And it's
always a storied spell of her life. I like
The details. The salad dressing she had
On the side. How many steps she's walked
Today. Since yesterday, not much has changed.
But little things have. One day, I might not
Have this simple bright thing, and I think,
No wonder everyone loves this woman.

Listen to her! On the other end
of the line. I tell her it's stormy where I am.
That I just left work—knowing my story
Is never as good as hers. There's a flash
flood watch here, she tells me, with urgency
In her voice. I start to say something, but instead
I listen for the sound of her voice.

May 25th

Late last night I thought I'd lost the cat.
I called and called to her
For an hour until, right before I went to bed,
I heard the bell on her collar ringing
From the neighbor's yard. She came in
Running, and groggy, as if she'd been
Napping for hours on someone's porch,
A little alarmed by her moonlit sprint in the dark.
The summer heat has arrived and we sleep
With the window open. Each morning
We hear the sound of birds waking
And soaring around the yard, scouting
For breakfast. I know how rare this happiness is.
Can I let it be without looking right at its brightness?
I know any minute it could slip away,
Or disappear. When you've lived your life
In a red panic. When you've worked
Endlessly, trying and failing, then find
Out, you're OK, that life has calmed down
For once, you can't help but take a moment—
To find a space—to call it what it is.
And if you can't name it. You can write
To it if you write a poem that feels more
Like a prayer. To not abandon the good,
Write down the richness as if sketching
Your new surroundings. It's what I have
To do: make a map to this place I found.
And it's OK if I can't recall everything,
Even as I wake, I reach for the same peace
The birds must know as they announce
Themselves to the coming day.

May 26th

Even in this time of completion
I feel the presence of silence.
The absence a reduction
Of all these missed letters,
Every poem is a retelling
Of the life you left. The question
Becomes should I bury this
Aqua notebook and keep these
Poems alive only to me?
No, the old words beg me back.
Won't you be braver, at the end?
Better? They say birds
Are the daughters of the air
And when I tell others I don't
Care, there's a part of me
That breaks off from the whole,
Damaged. Done in once again
By the past, and you, and me.

May 31st

Was there ever anyone more interesting
Than Saint Catherine of Siena?
A young girl promises herself to God
And a whole family erupts to doubt her.
Can't you see the 14th century room
Where the girl at wit's end, announced to them
What she planned to do? She even
Wrote a speech to steady her mind,
And as she broke the news to them,
That as a young girl she had promised
Herself to God, their faces fell. Questions
Soon began. Her father said it was all
A teenage tantrum. Determined to live
Her life by prayer, she cut off her light
Brown hair, devastating her mother.
The girl built herself a cell, slept
On wooden boards. A diet of bread
And water. What I mean is: some days
I can't believe in anything. But today
I'm reading about a girl who dug graves
For those who died from the plague.
There is a fury to this love, a good madness
In the strong will of a woman. A dove rests
Weightless in the air. It doesn't care
About my prayers. It never begged me to believe.

June 1st

I know I'm not the first person
To see the poetry in the center
Of gravity toys and pinhole cameras
That line the hallways of the university's
Chemistry-Physics building. But the soundless
Scope is so resonant here
In the summer. The halls have fallen
Quiet, left a peace-keeping white.
I find this summer silence again
And again, dressed in brightest maple;
Tones of blonde and white. Unused instruments
Now deep in their retirement—
You can tell. The ancient book
On Mechanics and Heat is stored
Behind a display case of thick glass,
A plate of dust catches in the light.
Why do I love this vacancy and left lot
Of rust and metal, lost in the folds
Of time? A gyroscopic balance rests
On the shelf above it all. The pages
Of a 19th century German manual
Are clipped and curling on the edges.
Here, in the lost season,
The equilibriums dip to the side
Even as the description for the helio-
Stat states, "in good working condition."
The old scientific instrument collection
Remains in the same sleepy corner
Of light. We'll go on living, like this.
All these relics of the past, watch
And wait. I've been here all this time.

June 4th

We walk together, on nights like this,
The dog always in front. There's a soft hush
As our footsteps part the tall grasses
Grown high this spring. In the distance, a light
Blinks off. Always, the same path, and each home
Casts a small glow. In one room, there's a lamp
Left on low. A fog has settled over
The soccer field, and a single runner
Runs past us, then the air empties of sound
We loop the green field of the high school,
And I talk to the dog as if she can hear,
Or respond. We go on, walking on nights
Like this, and there's not a lot to say.
Mostly, it's a matter of seeing
Past the shadowed phantoms of the trees.
She's alert to some unmistakable scent.
The past, always catching up to us.
I take a step and ask the air *who's been
Here?* Together we imagine who was.

June 9th

The summer days are so full. The world leaves
The city. You're gone, too, and I'm alone reading
About cognitive development theory on the same day
Clinton wins the democratic nomination. I am thinking
About what I want to say about this theory that Bode
And the Gestalt psychologists arrived at: that our past
Has an impact on how we learn. How we either know
Something or we don't. There's no gray area. I agree
That we come to see the solution when we spend time
Away from the problem. The eureka moment. I know
That moment. Tonight I made time to watch the evening
News because I wanted to see this historical moment
And let myself feel more of the pride I've been keeping
to myself. The wild wish rose in me. Life, you're about
To make sense. I sat there, watching her on the TV,
Feeling more than I knew I would. The mystery
Lifted in me as I sat there, alone, with history.

June 18th

After a week of tears and gunfire
The afternoon sun has settled lazily
On the hillside, illuminating three ruby-headed
Finches, dancing on a dry branch
Of the spruce tree. A burst of wind
And their tiny voices cry out
In unison. Are they about to die?
Or are they just having too much fun?
They flutter, nearly fall
Before rising, to land once again
On the branch they seem to love
So much, despite how dry and weak
This tree is. Parched from the heat,
It's no longer the hunter green it once was
And so, it's a surprise to me to see the new
Life so determined to make a home
Among those broken branches,
As if that place could still provide
Any kind of safety.

June 21st

There's a feeling that hangs in the air
After the summer storm has passed:
A single rabbit returns, then another,
Tentative from the far side of the tree.
A cardinal appears and calls out
An assurance that we can return
To our previous existence. No one
Believes me. The sky was dark
And lit with anger just hours before.
A mood so deadly and forlorn
We stood trapped in awe for once
And a silence came over us
As we considered the power
That held us fixed in wonder.

June 29th

Beneath me: a summer pit of red clay dirt.
I look out a window and see white pipes
The size of playground slides
Worming through the dirt, installed
In the earth, ready for a place
That's not been built. Everything
Has been lifted, moved, uncovered.
The world in open heart surgery. The world,
Hurt. Its caves dip in and out. The men grab
Their shovels. These diggers of the world
Are all leather gloves and hard-hats,
Hoping to make the world new
And futuristic. They have an idea
Of what it will look like: it will look like
A place they've seen in their dreams.
I see all these changes: the blasting of a sidewalk,
The new bricks replacing stonework
In an old facade, and yet I remember
The doorframes; how all the marbled pieces fit
Together, even if everything that was is now
Scattered into bits, like a broken pitcher
On the ground. Who wanted this
Transformation? I wanted the transformation.

July 4th

Deep in this holiday: silence
And the itch to say something.
A home sits lost in the rain, wondering
If anyone will come again. Maybe you.
Maybe you before you. I dream
And time passes as the day rests
Under a cloud of warm air. We go
Breathless and wrestle with the weight
Of it. Far off, the early spark of a firework
Breaking through the thunder
As people drive fast in their cars.
Where are they going? All the stores,
For miles, are closed.

July 11th

After days of not being
Able to say anything,
An image comes dressed
In the color of the earth itself.
Call her goddess. Call her
Girl in an army green gown
Facing a firing squad.
In the distance, a crowd,
And I can imagine
The roar and their fear.
What else is there? Guns,
Tears. Hands clapping for peace.
Prayers and water. The rest
Of the world watches us
Hurt each other through hate.
Let's find a new place
And write a new poem
Out of this shaken world.
Please? I'm a believer
In its terrible beauty.

July 21st

This evening a cool air broke
In, releasing the heat and rain-
Heavy air. It reminded me to be
Awake and ready for life to sweep
In, erasing the hazy days
That led you to hazy weeks
And yet, nothing changed, but me,
Standing there, thinking about life
Through the eyes of a poem.

July 29th

The house just down the road
From mine is rented by three guys
Who park their Dodge Rams
And Toyota pick-up trucks in a row,
Flattening the grass of their front yard.
They make it impossible to get past.
Deep grooves dug by their tires
Fill with rainwater whenever it rains
And their yard ripples with grooves of mud,
The uneven earth, sprinkled with trash.
Here and there, an empty beer bottle,
A pen cap. Maybe a tattered receipt.
There's a brown patch of earth, that's been
Burnt from some fresh spritz of Round-Up.
It's been choked of all breath, the bodies
Of dead flowers and grass fall in a colorless.
Silence. Tonight, as I walked past,
One of the men came out of the front door
Of the house wearing a shirt that said *Keep Calm
And Carry Guns* just as I was trying to find
A way to the other side. It must have looked
Like I was trying to hide, slipping between
The trucks on their lawn, not wanting to
Confront anyone. No, more often these days
I want to run from something I can't name.
Maybe it's everything. I was glad he turned
To go without seeing me standing there,
Feeling unforgivable in their yard
As my feet sunk into the dead Earth.
In my head, I apologized for the sounds I made.

August 4th

I turn around to call for her, only to find
Her missing, just as the sun is setting.
Even the hot wind is cooling
To a pale indigo. The day is soft
As breath, yet I can't help but think
Of winter rounding the corner.
It would find me in the middle
Of a field, with a pack of dogs
Running in little tornados
At my feet as a meadowlark
Flies past, a few feet away from me,
Soaring to the woods. My eyes follow
Along in flight. It's then I spot her
White tail through the vines of
Queen Anne's Lace and holly.
She leaps out of the woods,
Breaking out of the blackness
And into the final twitches of light.
And from the way she runs to me
I know she knows me, or has seen
Something back there, in the dark.

August 7th

For months we watched the blue spruce
Grow brown and speckled. The image blurred
Before us. We wondered if the last winter
Had finally killed the tree: the hard April freeze,
The July summer heat. It was my mother
Who examined the tree, diagnosing
the problem: Bag worms were taking over
Branch by branch, suffocating the trunk.
The tree stood taller than all of us. The three
Of us stood there, examining the tree,
Regarding it for maybe the first time.
I pulled a leafy vine away from its spine
And plucked one of the bag worms
From the branch, feeling it's flesh burst
Between two fingers, as the other three
Or four hundred hung on the branches
Giving the softest movement, in the wind,
Like tiny, unpainted ornaments.

August 11th

This morning I crossed Rose street, walked
To the median, and headed to the other side
Of campus, to a place I never go. I didn't expect
To see the early streams of water cascading
Down the lanes, the kind my dog loves to find
On our longest walks, in the summer.
The men were busy watering the violets
And begonias in the early light. People were beginning
Their Thursday crossing roads with coffee.
Some women wore sunglasses. Some people
Were smiling in a way that made me wonder
What they were thinking about. What
Were they smiling about as they walked
To work, likely in the exact same way
They did each day. Maybe they, too,
Were like me, in a place they knew
By heart, but going somewhere different,
For once. Being glad for the unknown,
Small change that awaited them, there,
In a place just out of view. Whatever it was,
They seemed to like the mystery of the beginning
That exists at the core of every morning. How the day
Invites us in with only a hint of what's to come.

August 14th

The Norton book on hand tools
Quickly reminds me of my father:
A life of dusty warehouses, of welding
And sawing. I was told to never touch
The creosote posts, and as a small child
I stayed outside, hiding out in the rows
Of stacked pressure-treated lumber.
I watched as the men in forklifts zoomed
Around, loading the orders into trucks
And trailers. I stayed outside after school,
Waiting for my mother to get off work,
While my father stayed late, calculating
Estimates and jobs. I still remember
The level, which he always kept so many of.
One, in particular, was always in his passenger
Seat. Climbing up, into that giant truck,
I always had to move the level out of the way
Before I got in to go anywhere with him.
He never said a word to me when I did.

August 21st

Three bags were taken inside:
Zucchinis, cucumbers, heirloom
Tomatoes, split and speckled
With dark clumps of dirt. I fill
Two sinks, plug the drains,
Placing the twenty-two tomatoes
In the low basin of water, watching
As they begin to wobble
And bob in the cool water.
With a yellow-gloved hand
I pop their caps off, rubbing away
The soil and mossy leaves.
The water clouds and browns
With soupy earth that
Spotted each plant
Plucked from the vines.
So strong and alive. And now?
Each one five shades of red,
Yellow, purple, and green
Now scrubbed clean
In the afternoon light, they
Sing their approximate
Loveliness through the silence
of late summer. Me, too, I think
Standing there at the sink.
My eyes rise to find an unexpected
Light flooding in from the outside.

August 25th

Light is narrowed and subdued
As we take the elevator down
To your appointment.
An hour later, I'm behind glass,
Holding a woman's hand,
Watching your surgery.
There, in the holy quiet,
Each of your eyes is magnified
On the screen, and I can't
See you, just each eye, big
As a basketball. Here, in the dark,
I am seeing that the past
Has caught up to the spectacle
Of us. And I think about all
The times I tried to describe
The color of your eyes: an ever-
Shifting swirl of blue and green.
The color always reminded me
Of the city of Charleston,
and the quick feeling of sun
And sand that lay in that sea-foam
Haze. The blue sky; a bright beach.
But now I see the brown center
Radiating out in rays of color.
The earth is inside the ocean
Is what I tell myself, to tell you
Later. Each eye, I'll tell you,
Looked just like a picture
Of Earth, but I know this
Isn't quite right, but it's
The closest thing I can say
When what it felt like was
Having all you love and everything

You fear stare into you. Like
Somewhere through the glass
Lay the constant mystery of us.

September 1st

This morning, their bodies woke early
Preparing for the trip they received
As a wedding gift. It has me thinking
About how surprising life can be,
Counting up the years since I knew
That what existed between the two
Of them was real. How I fought
The logic and the new order. But time
Has crept in and burrowed deep
Within me. Today they will arrive
In a pastel city beside the ocean,
And a tropical storm brewing
In the west will send waves of wind
Through the palm trees. How I want
This to be a love poem,
To celebrate all they are, but even
Now, the bright lights and tropical sun
Seem dipped in an orange haze, as
If steadying themselves in a sky
That still recalls the violet shift last night.

September 4th

This Sunday, a celebration:
Our nine year anniversary.
At the Holly Hill Inn, we look
Out over the lawn, dotted
With small butterfly gardens.
Each table houses a cocktail
Or two. The glasses bubbling,
And the blueberries bob
Like bubble tea. There's a quiet
Reflection to the day. We remember
Where we were ten years ago,
After the wreck. I had just graduated
College, unsure of my passage
From classes to graduation,
And then, my first real job.
We're left lingering in a radiant stillness,
Overhearing pieces of conversation.
Our eyes drifting to the lawn, imagining
Who we were, deciphering the silence
Between us. Is it a comfort, or something
Else? After all this time together, the story
Back then still roots itself in the new.

September 8th

We remember what Park City felt like
Nine years ago: the 1950s model
Car that took us away, after the wedding,
To the Cave City Convention Center.
All that shouting, the tiny lights strung up
To create a darkened path, and you, silently
Shocked by the love of those around you.
The guests, all hidden in a garden of blue
Hydrangea and bows, sky blue candles
Huddled and silk centerpieces. No one told
Us that marriage means color. That mostly it's better:
This way being surveyed and awake to everything
About the other person. And yet, you don't
Know what will become of each other. You never
Do. For example, I don't know who you will be,
though I still want a guarantee that we'll be
Stronger. No one else knows how we nearly fell
Apart a dozen times—some days held together
With strong rope and a couple knots, handled
Delicately on some days, other times, not.

September 9th

The rain garden was made by the Landscape Architecture
Students. They carved its mouth of water into the earth,
Planting switchgrass at the head. The foreground fills with more
Water, and I can imagine the horticulture team working together
On a sunny day, just like this, noticing the dipping land,
The stagnant water, imagining how they could give shape to this
And that. I stepped from the pavement to the grass, wanting
To get a better look at the group of plants that dwarfed the others,
A matter of water and compost he said. We eyed the water,
Thought about where it rests. I could make out the cracked land
Underneath the water. Beyond me, the barn rose up from the green.
The design studio was filled with students. Inside, there were notes
On infographics, ideas pasted to walls. Everything, a story. Above me,
A vaulted ceiling of wooden beams rose twenty feet in the air—etched
With memories, blond and copper lit with light. The students
Stare off into white paper, finding a narrative to echo the imagined field.

September 15th

Alone in the dark, we drive through the night,
Listening to the classical station break in
And out, Beethoven glimpsed, and missed
In large and small acts of crashing violence.
I wonder what you're thinking about, so·quiet.
Maybe you're lost, too, in the dark swell that's
Devoured us. No one asks anything. The dark,
A near blindness, to me, on nights like this. Leaving
The city for the country you notice how sweeping
The dark is. And now, I'm no longer a girl. No longer
Of this place. I find myself holding on, bracing
For something I cannot name, as if I need to be
Ready for the animal to break out of the forest
That surrounds us. I don't know what happened
To make me sure that the yellow tunnel of light
That's ours will be some tragic bait for the invisible
Animal, that waits in stillness, looking for us on nights like this.

September 24th

Here, at Wing Haven, fireplaces
Mingle with long forgotten benches.
Branches buckle and crack
Among the laughing children.
It's a place that was built
By hand, a vision married
To bird baths and love-in-the-mist.
I follow a trail to the Madonna
Fountain where I consider
The story of the founder, a woman
So at one with nature that birds
And the occasional rabbit
All made her house their own.
A home for whoever needed one.
A family of bluebirds lived there, too,
Took refuge in Shakespeare,
They liked the binding, found
The book strong enough to build
Their nest on. From there, they
Watched visitors come and go
Through the Victorian home.
When they weren't in the bookcase,
They could be seen landing on her
Arms as she played piano,
Delighted with the way her arms
Soared and danced to the song
She played. To them, it must
Have felt like music was something
They rode in the waves of her bones.

September 29th

Tonight, I looked up and the sky was lit
In waves of orange flames, dipping in and out
Of swirling indigo clouds. The light fell softly
Through the autumn shadows. At dusk, the slow hour
Cools every living thing, whispers, *this is our best
Chance* in a way that only you can hear.
There's a dampness to the night that wasn't here
Yesterday. The pep band plays for the football game
Down the street. The drum line announces itself
To the stadium and the evening draws a breath. I want
To tell you that all this is here, waiting for you.
Just when I think it won't be back, the music is in the air again.

October 6th

I've seen the way water
Gets into a place: crashing
At the sound. A harbor
Builds and builds until
A pool crowds out
The earth around us,
Enlightening the clouds.
The sky remains cool
And even. Unchanged
Despite the slow work
And continued drama
That breaks the earth.

October 8th

The Penobscot runs like a train rail
Around this city. Today we walked
Along Main, visited bookstores,
And made plans to set up camp
At Cumberland Gap or
Shenandoah in Virginia next year.
On this last day in Maine
We counted down the final hours
And minutes until we needed to be
Back at the Bangor Airport,
Where statues of moose
And pictures of Acadia
Decorate the walls. We're
Surrounded by miles of forests.
The landscape is in our veins.
Seeing the view from the riverbank,
Is something I've seen before. How is it
Still new to me? The land beneath my feet, a sturdy
World of permanence, and yet, I'm thinking
About the sharp, rocky edges I love so much.
Why am I drawn to the difficult? The drama
Of the beautifully broken?

October 12th

The Keurig will be the last to go.
Then, the rubberband ball,
The multicolor set of pens,
A stack of notecards, and the red
Ribbon around it. I'll take the silver
Water kettle, and the Chinese cup,
Pour out the water, and wipe out
The drawers. I'll grab the mints,
Pen caps, and oolong tea, take
The sugar and leave the post-it
Notes. How I loved the colorful
Ink, the swooping curves.
Each letter, a passing thought
Of the person I may see, someday
Looking up from my screen.

October 16th

In the pale blend of light
The dog races across the green
Like a galloping horse, careening
To the right, leaning into the sound
Of two voices. Here, all the dogs
Know each other as neighborhood
Friends. They catch up with each
Other on nights like this, the day
Slipping into dusk. We, the owners
Congregate in the green.
We talk to each other, but mostly
We're busy watching them roll,
And chase each other until
The moment they stop to shut
Their eyes and stare up in that
Secret way of theirs, like a form of praise.

October 22nd

When I walked out
To the clearing, three
Bird feeders strung up
On the low branches
Of trees, I could see
the place that would be
A space for you to rest
Under the leaves. I
Imagined the stones
At your feet as you
Assessed the distance
Between us. I could feel
The numerous silent weeds
Taking root in the wet
Earth, arrows along the path
That leads me to you.

October 24th

For weeks now, I've watched
The mother bird land
In the barren tree.
Landing on the bare branch,
Disappearing into the inner
Green core of what's left.
The spruce tree I let die
Needles me. I think of her.
What does she think of me?

November 9th

I pretend that this is the final day
in the year that robbed me of speech.
The day begins as a gray wall made
Of particulate mist. The gentle nod
To light that wakes from the corners.
I open the door to cold air, reminded
Of the long road ahead. Would I make
It? I barely know the way in my head.
There's a route we once talked about.
I'm thinking about it now. Remember
Those maps we got out, how the path
Was there before us, under
Our fingertips the blue and white lines
We could identify and pronounce.
And after we saw the way, we
Went to bed, picturing the way we had
Talked to each other when talking about
The way. Waking up alone, the stillness
Watching me invent the new day, I don't
See the new waves of light feeding into
The new day. I turn my back on what is
Left and I know I'm deep in something
I don't understand. Whatever it is, it's vast.

November 22nd

What do you say, when, after so
Long you begin to say it? Living,
Yes living, like we were. But we
Aren't what we were: patient
And viable, alive in the glass
Pearl of this world. The daze
Of questions and the rise
Of what we saw when we
Closed our eyes: yes, that's
What I'll remember. The real
Comfort of before and how no
One knew we were better,
Living as we were, flawed
In every way, yet we didn't
Panic. Tonight, sitting in the
Darkness, I remember that we
Were an idea, a belief that we
Were better as one.

December 1st

The day begins to fold inward earlier
And earlier, which made my discovery
Of the Purple-Crowned Fairy-Wren a moment
To savor. Imagine appearing a gem-
Stone to everyone you meet: monarch
Butterflies, June bugs, and garden snakes.
Imagine their black-eyed double-takes
As you soar around stealing the show,
The most pleasing thing in an ancient
Forest's memory. Your silky feathers:
Legendary. Yes, they must all want to know
About you, without really knowing
What it means, knowing you. The truth is,
They're already in love with the purity
Of your flight. They watch the beauty
Of your soft back as you leave their wondering
Faces. No, they don't know what you were,
But they'll remember how it felt to look up
And see you, a God racing among the leaves.

December 6th

The blue gray moves below—a heaven—
I watch winter resting on the expanse
Of greenhouses that lie out the window.
Rows of white, they rest at the periphery,
So solitary as they quietly breathe in
The winter air. How they obey whatever it is
In me that needs them to be there, standing
Still today. Almost respectful.
The world is in an uproar, the world
Has skipped ahead to its silent distress.
The coolness has again slipped over
The gold. And we now favor the silver
And white. I look out the window
At what's left: the rise of smoke
And steam. There's a far off heat rising
From the valleys that lie underneath.

December 13th

You say I match the stillness that's just
Beyond us. For years we've waited,
Watching as our city morphs into what's
Unrecognizable. We watch the steel
Buildings rise up past our shoulders.
We drive winter streets and begin to feel
Comfort in the lost way we feel. Maybe
Comfort is the wrong word. We each feel
Lost in our own way. And when there's
Nothing to say, we quietly stay together
As if waiting for the past to reach back,
like an old friend, and squeeze our hands.

December 21st

Even in darkness, the landscape
With its indigo outline of bone
Rises out of the winter fog
Whose breath of mystery shrouds
The dawn. I want to remember
The way the coldness transforms
The fog, (a thing we think we know),
Into a new beauty: chandelier ice
Or ice smoke. Crystals weighted
On the tree branches in perfect
Stillness, as if they, too, understand
The beginning and ending. How it's
Important, all this waiting. Meanwhile,
I tremble in the half-light, searching
The world for signs of a new dawn.

December 31st

On this road, the music swells,
Rising to meet me in the hills.
The violet heaven reaches
Down, pulling us into a new
Question: what was the original
Promise we made to each other?
I carry on, trying to be good
While sinking in the violence
And stories of violence, that
I can't seem to escape from.
We listen to the world bleeding
Itself to death. I lift the angel
From the tree, bending the white
Wing as it's sealed, and carefully put away.

OTHER ANAPHORA LITERARY PRESS TITLES

The History of British and
American Author-Publishers
By: Anna Faktorovich

Notes for Further Research
By: Molly Kirschner

The Encyclopedic Philosophy of
Michel Serres
By: Keith Moser

The Visit
By: Michael G. Casey

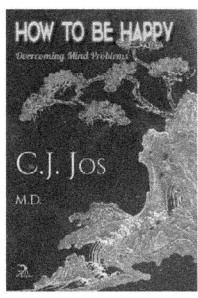

How to Be Happy
By: C. J. Jos

A Dying Breed
By: Scott Duff

Love in the Cretaceous
By: Howard W. Robertson

The Second of Seven
By: Jeremie Guy

CPSIA information can be obtained
at www.ICGtesting.com
Printed in the USA
BVHW030805130219
539975BV00008B/6/P